M000079333

Moments

Magic, Miracles, and Martinis

May your
path be
paved with
magic and
miracles!
Amy :)

PRAISE FOR *MOMENTS*

Amy's vulnerability, passion, and resilience is inspiring. She captures the truth and reality of life, while providing essential tools for growth and healing.

> – ALEXA SERVODIDIO, LCSW, TV & Radio Host,
> Author of *Finding Your Peace Within The Chaos*

The source of advice is sometimes more valuable than the advice itself. This is a book filled with firsthand knowledge on what it's like to fall, recover and stand again written by someone who's been there, done that and is now passing it on.

> – ALLYN REID, Mrs. San Diego 2015, Co-Founder
> Secret Knock, Publisher at Sherpa Press

Several years ago, Amy Van Atta Slater took the 24-hour challenge—the invitation to go twenty-four hours without complaining, about anything. And that decision changed her life. That is one of the many powerful stories Amy shares with us that inspires us to elevate our states—to upgrade our interpretations of our realities—and as a consequence, to upgrade, dramatically, our experience of life.

Amy is a model of positivity, authenticity, and personal transformation. Her stories will inspire you to move beyond your own fears and uncertainty. Each page of Moments *will touch your heart and soul. I couldn't recommend it more highly.*

> – CHRIS DORRIS, Mental Toughness Trainer
> and Personal Transformation Coach

Amy inspires and reminds us that the seeds of wisdom to deal with life's many curveballs all lie within us. She gives us a new word, thinkronicity, to realize the power of our thoughts to change our path.

> – NATASHA LEGER, Keynote Speaker, Author of
> *Healthy: A Road Warrior's Guide to Eating Healthy*

Moments - Magic, Miracles, and Martinis *is a beautiful journey of the soul; from adversity, uncertainty and self-doubt to inviting miracles, magic and a new way of being into your life; Amy Van Atta Slater guides you to powerfully move forward no matter how hard it gets with real relatable stories from her own life, a dash of magic, a stash of deep wisdom and of course a dirty martini or two! I loved this!*

    – MARINA J, Relationship Expert & #1 International bestselling author of *Turn Yourself On*

Humans love to learn through story and what better story to learn from than Amy Van Atta Slater's own journey to enlightenment. This book is the perfect vehicle for anyone who faces uncertainty, fear, shame or feelings of being unloved. It's also a wonderful roadmap for those 'believers' who are looking to reignite the magic they know exists, or remember how it feels.

As Amy shines the spotlight on the good, bad and ugly of her life, we are not uncomfortable or embarrassed for her because she is no longer in a place where that matters. As students, we are clearly able to see her growth and, if we wish, we can model her behavior.

Not once does she tell us how we 'MUST' live our lives, bark orders to 'DO as I Say' or Point a Finger' at us for our shortcomings, like so many other self help books.

No, Amy so cleverly 'packages the goods' by weaving possibility, positivity and passion through her own life examples, that we come away wanting to feel the way she feels, live our own authentic selves as she has, and most importantly, learn to love ourselves and open up to the wonderful possibilities that exist for us on the 'other side' of doubt and fear!

Get ready to LIVE in Your Moments, experience Your Magic and maybe, just maybe, (if you want) have a Very Dirty Xtra Dry Martini waiting for you when you arrive!

– FRANKIE PICASSO, Founder of *The Good Radio Network*, and Radio talk show host of *FrankieSense & More*, and *Mission Unstoppable Radio*

In life we sit and we wonder what it would be like to not be our true selves. I don't believe there is a soul on earth who does not wake up, look at the door and wonder what it would be like to open it to a new and exciting journey—to rid life of its natural complacency. As we reach a certain age we question our life's purpose, for me this is more and more apparent as I head into my 60's. The bold, and personal question, of "what if" I opened the door and walked through it (not just opened it) with the courage to embrace this magnificently scary and awesome universe, without fear and without expectations—what would happen to my life?

Moments: Magic, Miracles, and Martinis *answers the "what if", to remind us that fear is not a reason to stop truly living the only life we have. That love is not an excuse for being trapped. That miracles do happen, to all of us. And that magic is real, we need just open our eyes. Amy doesn't try "too hard" to write a book of tales, or wisdom, or how to get your spiritual groove on, but a book that inspired me to believe—to believe in myself.*

– WENDI COOPER, Owner & CEO of C *Spot Run* Productions, LLC

Moments; Magic, Miracles, and Martinis *is a soulful and insightful read. Each chapter is a link to creating a better you! Read with an open heart!*

– SAM TOOLE, Producer

I am sure I speak for the entire team when I say that we are lucky to have had Amy as our coach. The final touches and tweaks to the presentation, her encouraging remarks before the presentation, and the little tips here and there helped all of us do a better job, no matter how stressed we were. With Amy's guidance we took a calculated risk—which everyone I spoke with agreed paid off. I am very proud of what we accomplished as a team!

— KHALIL HAJ-KHALIL, Engineering Director, Burbank

Moments

Magic, Miracles, and Martinis

HOW TO MOVE FORWARD
IN TIMES OF UNCERTAINTY

Amy Van Atta Slater

TURTLE SPIRIT PRESS  CORTE MADERA, CA

MOMENTS: *Magic, Miracles, and Martinis*
Amy Van Atta Slater

© 2016 Amy Van Atta Slater

Published by Turtle Spirit Press, Corte Madera, CA
www.turtlespiritpress.com

Cover and book design: Chris Molé Design
Copy editor: Deborah Mokma
Photos: © Charles Schoenberger Photography

Cartoon credits:
Snapshots, page 39 © 2015 cartoonstock.com

Olive & Twist, page 63: © 2015 Grimmy, Inc.
Distributed by King Features Syndicate, Inc.

ISBN: 978-0-9970700-1-9
Printed in the United States of America
10 9 8 7 6 5 4 3 2 1

Dedicated to the dear ones who made
the moments magical:

My three amazing daughters
Megan, Alyson, and Jordan.

And to my parents, John and Pam Van Atta,
who model unconditional love and respect.

TABLE OF DISCIPLINES

How to move forward in times of uncertainty.

FOREWORD

During times of uncertainty, challenges and change, how do we find a ray of hope to move forward? In *Moments: Magic, Miracles, and Martinis,* Amy bears a torch of inspiration, motivation, mindfulness and authenticity that illuminates even the most desperate of situations with possibility.

Amy bravely shares her struggles and challenges that so many people can relate to. With the end of her 17-year marriage, Amy was suddenly faced with the reality of not only having to go through a painful divorce proceeding, but her family would be broken up and she would be co-parenting her three daughters in a way that she had never considered. To make matters worse, Amy was dealing with an onslaught of issues arising from her Irritable Bowel Syndrome (IBS); her father, who was diagnosed with Lewy Body Dementia, was further deteriorating in his condition, and she started a new job that came with its own set of stresses. Insecurities crept in as she began to doubt herself. Instead of becoming immobilized with depression, sadness and fear, Amy used these difficulties to spark growth in her life in ways that she never dreamed possible.

With so much uncertainty and chaos in her life, Amy knew

that the only thing she could control were her thoughts and how she responded to what was unfolding around her. It was in her quest to find a more peaceful, meaningful and fulfilling life that Amy discovered by letting go of fear, she gained true freedom and liberation.

Often it is said that through life's greatest tragedies, our greatest triumphs are realized. As a highly recognized Sales Leader in Fortune 500 companies and a catalyst for change and innovation, Amy looked to see how she could implement the same techniques that made her so successful in her business life, translatable to her personal life.

With an open heart and mind, Amy shares the simple truths she uncovered that will move you through any situation with grace, gratitude, authenticity and peace.

MARIANNE PESTANA - Radio show host at
Moments with Marianne Dreamvisions 7 Radio
Network & WMEX 1510AM Boston

INTRODUCTION

"When you want something, all the universe conspires in helping you to achieve it."

– PAULO COELHO, *The Alchemist*

One day I decided: I am going to write a book. Then, I declared to the Universe and to those kind enough to listen, "I am writing a book." It became clear to me over time that the book would be governed by whatever happened, and I discovered that there is an uncanny comfort gained when you declare you are going to do something but do not need to know *any* of the details. There is also incredible power in declaring that you are going to do something when you do not know much about it, and it appeared the stories were spontaneously written by virtue of my declaration.

This reminds me of the time, five years ago, when I decided to run a marathon—decided *and* declared that I would run a marathon. I was dozing off in bed one evening while flipping channels when I stopped at *The Biggest Loser* program, which was in its final phase with the contestants running a marathon. I watched in awe as they dragged their tired, aching bodies across the finish line. I said to my husband, "Wow, I could never do that!"

"Why do you say that?" he asked. "I am sure you could if you put your mind to it." That was exactly what I was afraid of in that moment. If I put my mind to it, I would have to do it. I figured I could train my body, but it was the mental toughness that accompanies the training and commitment needed to run a marathon that really concerned me.

Within moments, I decided (well, we decided) we would run a marathon. Two days later we registered for the San Diego Rock 'n' Roll Marathon, and within a few days after that had our "do it yourself" marathon book, *The Non-Runner's Marathon Trainer*, in hand. Little did I know that once I declared it to others, I would be "all in," and there would be no turning back: In declaring it, I was one step closer to finishing it.

I am happy to say that I ran that marathon on June 7, 2010 (almost five years ago to the day of this writing), and I joined the .5% of Americans who have also run a marathon. And, that was it. I have probably run less than 26.2 miles since that race, and instead am happy hiking, walking, and enjoying a slower, softer pace.

Not long after checking running a marathon off my bucket list, I embarked on a different journey—another marathon of sorts. Just three months following our hand-in-hand limp across the finish line, my husband and I decided to join a different population; not only had we finished a marathon, we had also crossed the finish line of our marriage.

Twelve months later, the sobbing that escaped my once stone façade broke the silence of my empty house. Where did the dream go? How did I get here? Alone. Empty. Defeated. Afraid. Divorced. It took me a long time before I could even mouth that word.

D-i-v-o-r-c-e-d

How could I let down my family? *'Til death do us part,* right? My parents had been married for fifty-one years, and they were always incredible role models. I felt like a failure, unable to make my own marriage work after all these years. Now, I thought, my three beautiful daughters are just another statistic of a "broken" home. I was overcome with fear and uncertainty as I imagined the road ahead.

> *"Grief and pain are like joy and peace; they are not things we should try to snatch from each other. They're sacred. They are part of each person's journey. All we can do is offer relief from the fear: I am all alone."*
>
> – GLENNON DOYLE MELTON, *Carry on, Warrior: Thoughts on Life Unarmed*

Whether or not you initiate divorce, it sucks. There is no way around it. It just plain sucks. You don't walk down the aisle thinking, "Oh, if this doesn't work out, I will just get divorced. No big deal." Well, it *is* a big deal. What I have learned in the last four years, however, is that it is what *we* make of it. We are the story we create. Each of us is responsible for the evolution of our own narrative, which is why I wrote my own collection of stories about the journey and awakening I experienced following my separation, and ultimate divorce, after seventeen years of marriage. My intention here is not to write about the divorce or why it happened, or to place blame, shame, or hurt on anyone. My goal is to share how miraculous my life has become since breaking down the protective wall I had constructed. Perhaps through sharing my journey, you too can be blessed with miracles that are merely masked by your own fear, and can more comfortably face the uncertainty that awaits you on your journey.

CHAPTER ONE

Cry

"When you transform your whole dream, magic just happens in your life. What you need comes to you easily because spirit moves freely through you."

– DON MIGUEL RUIZ, *The Four Agreements*

Needless to say, following divorce we all have the desire to feel wanted again. We go through phases of self-pity, self-destruction, and, ultimately, if we're lucky, self-discovery. It is easy to lose control of one's life. We can go from having a plan, and a pretty clear future, to "Oops!" when it feels like the rug has been pulled out from beneath you. Everywhere I turned, I was reminded that I was alone. I was one. School registration documents highlighted the fact that I was indeed divorced. And there was the ever-present Marital Status on so many forms: single, married, or divorced. Really? Did I have to tell the world that I was a failure? *I failed marriage.* Please don't remind me, I thought.

My first order of business was to prevent loneliness. I had too much spare time on my hands now that my girls were only in the house 50% of the time, so I did whatever I could to fill the void. I was out more than I was in (literally and figuratively). My fear of loneliness caused me to work too much, go out more, and avoid silence at any cost—because it was then that all I could hear were my own thoughts banging around in my head. I cycled through all too many "what ifs" and "if onlys," but that kind of thinking made me crazy, so keeping busy gave me a good excuse to ignore those nasty voices in my head.

Part of the healing process was to go out and at least appear less alone, and I did what many newly unattached people do by joining an online dating site. Boy, can that make you feel artificially popular! The irony is, despite all of the dates, I felt even more alone, but will avoid going through the litany of failures and unthinkable circumstances that arose. Thanks to one of the dates, however, I was given an amazing gift, and while I did not find the man of my dreams online (despite my initial fascination with that idea), I did find a man who was able to unlock my deepest dreams through his thoughtful sharing of a YouTube TED talk.

A few days following our one and only dinner date, my new friend sent me an Internet link (**www.ted.com/talks/ brene_brown_on_vulnerability?language=en**). Little did I realize that this twenty-minute video would forever change the trajectory of my life.

Seated on the couch with my always-reliable laptop companion, I clicked on the link. If I were to play this out in a movie, you would hear music building as my fingers timidly touched the keys, uncertain of what was about to unfold before me.

The big, red TED letters flashed across the screen as I waited for the video buffering to stop—I mark this moment as the beginning of my journey of miracles. The video that began to play was that of Brené Brown, author and "social anthropologist."

Within seconds of her opening monologue, I was riveted on the edge of my seat with tears streaming down my face. Her words spoke directly to my heart and soul, piercing what I had thought was an impenetrable wall around every part of my being. She spoke of vulnerability; she spoke of authenticity; she spoke of shame. With every word, the sobs became deeper and deeper. My heart pounded faster and faster. How did she know me so well? She spoke of courage. She spoke about our incessant self-doubt and fear of not being good enough, or rich enough, or smart enough. Boy, did those words sound hauntingly familiar.

"There was only one variable that separated the people who have a strong sense of love and belonging and the people who really struggle for it. And that was, the people who have a strong sense of love and belonging believe they're worthy of love and belonging. That's it. They believe they're worthy. And to me, the hard part of the one thing that keeps us out of connection is our fear that we're not worthy of connection."

– Brené Brown, TED.com

When the video ended, I sat there in utter silence. Only this time, in the silence, I no longer felt alone. Exhausted from the tears, somehow I felt different. I felt lighter. The protective wall I had architected around myself over a lifetime had crumbled at my feet. I began to question my own self-doubt and age-old struggle with trying to be perfect—the perfect daughter, the perfect wife, the perfect mother, the perfect friend, and the perfect employee. I realized this striving for perfection had only left me feeling terribly defeated and "not enough." The words of Brené Brown gave me permission to be vulnerable, and the courage to believe that I am *enough*.

"Authenticity is the daily practice of letting go of who we think we're supposed to be and embracing who we are. Choosing authenticity means cultivating the courage to be imperfect, to set boundaries, and to allow ourselves to be vulnerable; exercising the compassion that comes from knowing that we are all made of strength and struggle; and nurturing the connection and sense of belonging that can only happen when we believe that we are enough."

– BRENÉ BROWN, *The Gifts of Imperfection: Let Go of Who You Think You're Suppose to Be and Embrace Who You Are*

Although the wall had been broken down, I knew I had to repair and nurture my inner core to awaken the magic I was to find on my path ahead.

CHAPTER TWO

Stop Complaining

"Go 24 hours without complaining (not even once).
Then, watch how your life starts changing."

– Katrina Mayer, *The Mustard Seed Way*

Not long after the vulnerability wrecking ball knocked down that concrete wall around my soul, I was blessed with another close encounter of a new dimension. Raw and exposed, I felt that my awareness was at a much higher frequency. It seemed that someone (I will tell you who later) was pointing me in a new direction.

I was at a fairly new job at Salesforce.com when I had the opportunity to attend a fifty-person sales offsite in Scottsdale, Arizona. The group was large enough to generate tremendous energy, yet small enough for us to meaningfully engage. As the taxi pulled into the driveway of the hotel, I took several deep breaths of the dry desert air. I still had the tan line on my finger where my wedding ring had nestled for seventeen years, which in the past had provided a sense of security and belonging when I was away. But now, I was on my own.

On the first day of the offsite, we had a full agenda. Despite the Arizona heat, I sat shivering in the large conference room that was air conditioned down to a bone chilling temperature. Eight large tables filled the room, and I chose a table close to the exit in case I needed to make a quick get away. Once the seats were filled, the day rapidly unfolded and, even now, remains one of the most inspiring days of my life.

Our mental toughness coach, Chris Dorris, spoke for ninety minutes—which flew by like ninety seconds—as he spoke of being All In, moving toward what you want and deciding, declaring, and doing what it takes. While I can't do his stories and teachings justice, I can pass along one of the tools I took away with me, one that has unlocked a treasure trove of infinite magic, lightness, discovery, and teachings.

At the end of his talk, Chris posed the group with a challenge. He said, "I challenge each of you to go twenty-four hours without complaining. If you complain, you must start the clock over. As you do this, slow down enough to watch what happens." Well, I was never one to pass up a challenge, so I decided "why not?"

I left the hotel with a kick in my step and a smile on my face. Somehow, I felt better equipped to face the uncertain road ahead than when I had arrived just twenty-four hours prior. Chris's words replayed over and over again in my head: Move toward. Don't complain. Decide. Be All In.

On my quick flight home from Arizona, I read through Chris's website and listened to his *All In* CD. I felt well armed, ready to go back to work and face the reality that was waiting for me at home—which was going through a transformation of sorts now that it was just the girls and me. I had embarked on the 24-hour challenge, which was pretty easy to stick to when you are sitting alone on a plane. The real challenge comes when you walk back across the threshold to reality. I had yet to experience any magic that Chris promised would be on its way. I waited...

The next morning as I was getting ready to leave for work, I stopped in my tracks when I saw my oldest daughter (age seventeen) sitting in tears at the breakfast table, her head in her hands. "Honey, what's wrong?" She proceeded to share how sad she was that she and her high school boyfriend of two years were going off to out-of-state colleges and were breaking up.

Needless to say, her story tugged at my heartstrings. With the 24-hour challenge in the back of my mind I said, "I know how hard it is sweetie. Think how lucky you are to have experienced a love like this. Now, when you go off to college, you will know what to look for in a relationship. Some people never have that experience." Prior to the challenge, I would have gone down into the abyss with her and commiserated about how unfair life is. Not this time, however.

As I began to walk away, I wrote down Chris's website and suggested she watch the videos where he talks about mental toughness. As many teens do, she gave me a slight eye roll while mustering up a quiet "thank you."

Once at work, I received a text from her. Simply written, "I am what I create."

Was this the magic that Chris was talking about?

Later that morning, I received an email alert through my

LinkedIn account. The email came from someone who had worked for me fifteen years prior, when I was a young sales manager trying to find her way in corporate America. To this day, years later, I have saved his message, as it is another example of the magic that appeared during my challenge:

> *Amy,*
> *I want to tell you this, and you might not even care; but I need to tell you. You were a great person to work for and you really care about people. I never should have left LCI when I was working for you. I have three brothers who are a lot older than me, and I was trying to achieve the success they had without putting in the work and time. I was too immature to realize that you needed to work hard at a company and put in the time before looking for a new opportunity.*
>
> *Back then, it was a very confusing time in my life, and I should have sat down with you and discussed what was going on instead of jumping jobs.*
>
> *I just want you to know that I enjoyed your friendship and your compassion as my boss. I always thought you were an awesome person!*

I was nearly sixteen hours into my challenge, and I was starting to believe in the magic that Chris had alluded to the day before. Every time I heard someone complain at work, it sounded like nails on a chalkboard—people must have wondered what kind of drug I was on as I moved so effortlessly through my day. I also noticed how hard it is for others to complain when you don't engage in the complaining with them. After studying more about this phenomenon, I learned to describe it as rising up to a higher vibration. Positive energy begets more positive energy.

"With each progressive rise in the level of consciousness, the "frequency" or "vibration" of energy increases. Thus, higher consciousness radiates a beneficial and healing effect on the world, verifiable in the human muscle response, which stays strong in the presence of love and truth. In contrast, non-true or negative energy fields induce a weak muscle response."

– DAVID R. HAWKINS, *Power vs. Force*

Another way to describe this is to talk about the "O" line, or the line of observation. When I coach people or run sessions on influencing positive culture, I talk about staying above the "O" line, which happens when we use positive language and vibrations. We fall below the "O" line when we use negative words and thus lower the vibration. As an example, think about how we might describe the weather:

"O" Line: *It is 90 degrees today.*

"+" Above the O Line: *It is a spectacular, sunny day.*

"-" Below the O Line: *I am melting from this dreadful heat.*

Each of these phrases sets off different emotions and can be witnessed in a variety of discussions ranging from love to war. Years later, I am convinced that friends, family, and colleagues would describe me now as a very positive, "Above the O line" type of person. So much so, that people around me apologize when they themselves are being negative. They say things like, "I don't mean to be negative, but ..." My answer to them is, "then *don't* be."

CHAPTER THREE

Slow Down

"Dance like no one is watching. Sing like no one is listening. Love like you've never been hurt and live like it's heaven on Earth."

– MARK TWAIN

Keeping up with the pace of life can make it excruciatingly difficult to remain present. To-do lists multiply like an incurable fungus, and the ability to focus wanes as technology sucks me into a deep vortex. Balancing the demands of children, family life, and a more than full-time job had me spinning like a top on most days. I was wound very tight, yet my façade was one of strength, confidence, and ease as I plowed through the field ahead. Until I was forced to slow down and reassess my life, I thought this was normal, and I had no idea how to shape my future any differently.

And then, I woke up. Following my divorce it was as if the Universe kept redirecting me toward a new horizon. Subtle messages kept pulling me up, pulling me inward, reminding me to reflect and slow down. Slowing down allowed me to see things that I had never "seen" before, and I finally gave credence to the age-old cliché: "Stop and smell the roses."

As I reflect, it seems to me that slowing down created some of the greatest benefits in parenting. Just a few months ago, my youngest daughter (age ten) begged and begged to invite one of her best friends over for a sleepover. I was happy to oblige, as I know how special those times are in a child's life. We gathered all of the blankets, sleeping bags, and pillows, spreading them out on the family room floor in front of the large, flat screen TV. Of course, no slumber party is complete without popcorn and a movie, so we rifled through our various digital movie sources and settled on *Pitch Perfect*.

As a point of context, my daughter and her friend have known each other for years and, for better or worse, are both children of divorce. They give each other comfort in times of sadness, and feel safer taking this journey together. Her friend didn't leave her house for sleepovers very often, so this was a step outside of her comfort zone. Knowing this, I made sure to keep the energy high. Her mom had gone out for the night, and I wanted to preserve her time away.

About thirty minutes into the movie, I saw Chloe curled up on her side with her back gently heaving (a sure sign of crying). I kneeled down beside her and noticed little tears trickling down her rosy cheeks. My maternal instinct kicked in, and I gently rubbed her back. She cried and asked for her mommy, and I softly explained that she was out and perhaps we should wait a few minutes before calling her. My daughter sat with a concerned look on her face and said, "It will be okay.

When my mom is away, it helps me to imagine her. Then I feel better." She joined me in rubbing Chloe's back, and her tears gradually subsided. The girls turned their attention back to the movie, and I let out a quiet sigh of relief.

Just a few minutes later, we repeated the same scenario; only this time, I started to question if I was doing the right thing. Should I call her mother? Am I being too hard on this tow-headed little girl? Despite my inner self-doubt, I continued to caress her back and redirect the energy. In no time, the girls began laughing, singing, and engaging in a pillow fight. I left them to their fun and headed upstairs to get ready for bed.

Once upstairs, I sat on the edge of the bed. Listening to the laughter downstairs, I began to reflect and had flashbacks to ten years before, when I experienced something similar, yet different, with my middle daughter, now eighteen. She, too, had a sleepover with a tow-headed little girl, a typically rowdy little eight-year-old soccer friend who now had become withdrawn and shy. Her father had warned me that she often asked to come home, and to be sure to call him if she changed her mind.

Like the present scenario, we prepared the same family room with blankets, pillows, popcorn, and movies. I believed that if I made the evening busy enough, I could mask the worry and fears of this now quiet little friend. I managed to get the girls settled down enough to watch the movie, and I headed upstairs. Not long after putting the girls to bed, my daughter climbed the dark staircase to report that Tara was crying. I gave Aly a big hug, and tightly held her small hand as we walked down the stairs. Seated by Tara's side, I rubbed her back as she looked at me with her large, sad eyes and said,

"I want to go home. Can you call my dad?"

At this point you must be asking yourself why I am going to the trouble of sharing a second story about a simple sleepover, but I now realize a decade later what the true difference was: I CRUMBLED. I pushed the infamous, red, EASY button. I did not have the ability to simply sit with Tara in her sadness and hold space with her fear. Instead, I pulled the ripcord. It didn't matter that it was midnight, and her father would awaken to my soft whisper telling him that his daughter wanted to come home. Had I taken the time to comfort and soothe her, she might have gone back to sleep, and I now believe I had robbed her of a chance to learn how to soothe herself. Had I known what I know now about slowing down, I could have helped her more and modeled compassion and patience. Pico Iyer said, "The more we run from a problem, the more we're actually running into it."

My mind continues to wind through childhood memories and the impact that they have on who I am today. If we don't slow down, we may miss meaningful connections and lessons. When I am present, truly present, the teachings are infinite. One such memory inspired me to write the following blog that fits so well in this chapter on slowing down.

When In Doubt, Pause

First off, I have to say that I love being a mother. I don't mean to sound trite, but I really do love being a mother to my three daughters, although this isn't to suggest that it has all been champagne and roses.

Since my divorce four years ago, I have found more space and energy to be present as a mother. Because I have more time to nurture my spirit, I am available to my daughters in new and magical ways. I am consciously slowing down so that I can be mindful of what I say and of the lessons we can learn together. I cannot help but reflect on my experiences with my own mother when I am nurturing the relationships with my girls.

In fact, just the other day, my youngest daughter (age ten) starting talking about the "gifted" program at her school. She said that the kids that are not "smart enough" are left in the classroom while the "smart" kids go learn harder things. Needless to say, the hairs on the back of my neck stood up when I heard her describe it this way. I was quick to respond by telling her that it wasn't that she and the others are not smart enough, rather that the other kids are seeking additional challenges in school. This topic hits me deeper than most as I too lived through this as a young girl.

In my day, the "gifted" kids were pulled out from the classroom to attend what was called "Special Class." That, in and of itself, was a problem for me because it left the rest of us feeling not "special." As a child I had been pulled out of class for testing in the office, just to be told to go back to class because they weren't ready for me. I was to be tested for the special class, and the whole point was to make sure kids did not have time to anticipate the tests to avoid anxiety during the process. Well, that plan was dead on arrival since I was given a false alarm.

Hours later, when called back to the office, I was full of fear and anxiety. My fear of test taking was now exaggerated as I had time to stew about it. When I got to the testing, I answered questions before they were asked and was anxious through the entire exam. I can still remember the tests of patterns and blocks and numbers; the cold feeling I had in the sterile room next to the principal's office. Failure was not an option. Yet, sure enough, my score was not sufficient for placement in the special class, so I was, by default, NOT special.

Here is where the parenting lesson comes in. From the moment my mother found out about this, she wrapped me in her arms and said, "you ARE special." Now, it was not her words that have stuck with me all of these years, but rather her actions. You see, the kids in the special class had to arrive at school an hour earlier than the regular kids. And, of course, all of the kids I carpooled with were in the special class. That meant that once a week, my mom had to drive me to school without the others. On those days, my mom created a special class just for me. We would sit on the loveseat in our family room and read books on dinosaurs that we had taken a trip to the bookstore to purchase exclusively for our own special class. Those books were special. The time was special. My mom was special. And most of all, I felt special.

Fast forward forty years, and I still remember how I felt sitting beside my mom with a book in our lap. I think about this often.

It is easy to get swept away by the to-do's in our lives. Take the time to pause.

To listen.

To see.

To love.

I believe that being a mother is the most important and most rewarding job I will ever have.

The pause makes me a fully present mother.

I realize that slowing down is not just about parenting moments, but rather it is about *each* moment. On Father's Day 2015, I had the opportunity to spend the day with my seventy-six year old father in his nursing home. When I first visited him there several months prior, I was filled with fear and apprehension. How would I feel seeing him like this? How should I act? What should I say? I realize now that I wanted to get in and get out. Just like that—get it over with to run from the discomfort. So often, we want to escape from sadness and do so by moving quickly past the pain, leaving it as road kill in our wake. The unfortunate reality is that the pain does not actually go away, it is simply buried for us to dig up at a future date.

Now, on Father's Day, I managed to face my fears. My mom has a quote on her kitchen bulletin board that reads, "Courage doesn't always roar. Sometimes courage is the little voice at the end of the day that says I'll try again tomorrow."—Mary Anne Radmacher. This quote must have resonated with me on Father's Day as we read his cards aloud, and I gave him his Boston Red Sox sweatshirt. The look in his eyes told me that he recalled the Red Sox as his favorite team. He even tried to lift his arms as if to cheer as a devoted fan. We took selfies with my iPhone. After the first shot, he kept making funny faces at the camera as if seeing himself for the first time. I felt much like a parent does when seeing your toddler recognize himself in his reflection.

As we sat eating at the outdoor café, I fed him his pizza and Sprite. I carefully cut up the pieces of pizza and fed him with a fork. With one hand, I gently held his slightly shaky fingers and with the other, I carefully nudged the pizza into his open mouth. He gobbled up three pieces, grinning like a child between bites and sips of soda through a straw. I did not rush this time. I spoke to him about great childhood memories; we all laughed; we shared; we were present in the moment. I will cherish every last minute that I have with him and will no longer race by the sadness. Feeding my dad is as much for me as it is for him. We share time. One never knows when it will be the last moment, and I have decided to make each moment count.

Back at my mom's house that afternoon, we spoke of our time together with my dad. We continued to share stories and wonderful family memories. As we sat holding hands on the soft leather sofa, I realized that we were not grieving and anticipating his imminent passing—rather, we were celebrating his life. My mom's blue eyes twinkled as she spoke of the love of her life since the ripe old age of thirteen. She spoke of how grateful she is to have had so many wonderful years with him. Could it be that by raising the vibration of energy with my mom she was able to smile and laugh and live again? She commented how relaxed she was even with the known uncertainty of the path before her. In slowing down, we were able to be present together.

Fast forward a few weeks, and I was having dinner with my friend Nancy, with whom I have lived a parallel life in many ways. We each have three daughters, very close in age. Our oldest and middle daughters played competitive soccer together, and Nancy and I spent numerous weekends driving to tournaments around the Bay Area. These weekends were about more than sport. Nancy and I also spent hours on and off the field sharing life's ups and downs. At a certain point our friendship was transformed from "fellow soccer moms" to "moms going through stuff together," and, coincidentally, Nancy and I went through our divorces at the same time. Our divorces were so in sync that we shared the same Marin County court date for dissolution of our marriages. What are the odds of that?

Years later, Nancy and I have become closer than ever. We help each other through tough decisions regarding our girls and provide emotional support along the way. The other day, Nancy and I were having dinner and simply sharing our recent week's experiences, when she recounted her latest visit to a car dealership when her car was in need of repair. Nancy commented that this was the first time ever that she turned down the loaner car she usually used to make the most of every second while her car was being serviced.

On this occasion, Nancy walked into the waiting room and uncomfortably sat down in the stiff vinyl chair. Within seconds, an elderly woman sitting across from her smiled and kindly complimented her on her purse. That led to what Nancy describes as a precious conversation. Next, an employee came up and offered her coffee, water, and/or tea, and pointed out the well-stocked kitchen. She wandered into the kitchen where a soft-spoken gentleman struck up a conversation about the assorted teas. What unfolded was an interesting conversation about how the man's neighbors are so nice to his daughter with special needs. When Nancy sat back down, a gal in her mid-twenties arrived and struck up a conversation that turned to the subject of dogs. The stranger was thrilled to tell Nancy all about her new and successful dog walking business, and all the joy she gets out of it.

When Nancy's car was ready, over an hour later, she couldn't help but realize how great she felt. As she drove away, what struck her was the positive energy that was generated simply by MAKING THE CHOICE to SLOW DOWN. Instead of rushing off to do errands and multi-task while her car was being serviced, Nancy had stood still. Without any place to go or anything to do, she was forced to be there in the moment. Nancy says she will never forget the magic that transpired simply by slowing down and welcoming that rich, warm, and caring time with absolute strangers.

As Nancy's experience so beautifully illustrates, in slowing down we are able to sit with stillness and any inevitable discomfort that may accompany it. We instinctually speed through life to prevent ourselves from facing our fears. Slowing down takes courage. Slowing down means not taking the easy way out. Try it. Stop and smell the roses. Find beauty in the spaces in between: Coming and going, sunrise and sunset, open and shut. I promise ... you *will* find magic moments.

CHAPTER FOUR

Be Authentic

"We all have the capacity to inspire and empower others. But we must first be willing to devote ourselves to our personal growth and development as leaders."

– *Discovering Your Authentic Leadership*
GEORGE, SIMS, MCLEAN, and MAYER
Harvard Business Review

There was little I loved more than spending time with my dad alone, some of the most memorable of these occasions being when I accompanied him to his office in Van Nuys, California. At the time, circa 1976, my dad was larger than life. He had this way of seeing the world, not just with the glass half full, rather with the glass overflowing. I have a new appreciation for just how unique his perspective was, especially in a world that was all about keeping up with the Joneses and the fleeting American Dream. Today, I have a new language to describe him and his universal appeal, and I now realize that my dad was *authentic* before authenticity became cool.

When I would walk through the grand glass doors of the Carnation Research Lab in Van Nuys, holding on tight to my father's strong hand, I felt such pride in being the boss' daughter. The irony is that my father wasn't boastful about his job, nor did he expect people to revere him. He was Dad to me, so when I heard people say, "Good morning, Dr. Van Atta" I would look around for a medical doc in a white lab coat. In fact, the workers who greeted him were actually the ones in lab coats while my dad always went to work in a suit and tie, his shirt hand pressed by my mother (scenes of Leave it to Beaver or Ozzie and Harriett must be going through your mind).

The break room was always the first stop on these visits. The smell of freshly brewed coffee filled the room, the walls were lined with vending machines and the counters littered with near-empty donut boxes. What a sharp contrast to today's break rooms, that are lined with various organic coffees and teas that drip out of Keurig machines, one cup at a time. Break rooms used to truly be just that—a place to take a break. Now, they are places that people pass through as they mindlessly zip past one another, devices in tow with hardly a nod of hello.

Styrofoam cup in hand, my dad would escort me to the supply room. You'd have thought I was going to see the Wizard in the Wizard of Oz. A tall cabinet teemed with yellow legal pads, Bic pens, pencils, and small glistening bottles of White Out. In his booming voice my dad would say, "Pick what you want and follow me," and I'd frantically collect my supplies for the day, trailing after him in his wake. Dad would sit me down at the big round table next to his desk, tell me to make myself comfortable, and within minutes he'd be busy reading memos and fielding intercom calls from his secretary. I would sit there in awe as people came into his office to discuss business because he spoke with such confidence as he dished out advice to his eager employees.

At last, it would be time for lunch. On most days, my dad played volleyball in the rear parking lot of the lab, but in my honor we would eat in the cafeteria. That day, when we were walking through the narrow hallway, my dad stopped us in our tracks. I noticed a man a decade or so younger than my dad walking toward us. "Amy, I'd like you to meet George." I stuck out my tiny ten-year-old hand to shake George's strong hand as my dad continued, "George is the best pet food scientist there is, and we are lucky to have him here." Despite being a child, I knew pride when I saw it. George's eyes lit up like a Christmas tree when he heard those words from Dr. Van Atta. Years later when I, too, went into management, I remember recalling that story with my dad, who explained that he always wanted people to feel valued. To this day, nearly forty years later, I still hear from my dad's work colleagues who talk about the Carnation family and how he made them feel. What you saw was what you got with my dad who, today, sits in a wheelchair, in a nursing home as he lives with Lewy Body Dementia. Although he can no longer speak, he still has that twinkle in his eye and makes you feel like the most important person on the planet.

On occasion, I am lucky enough to bring one of my daughters to work with me. They may not have quite the same fascination that I once had, but they do like knowing where I spend my time. About a year ago, I had just such an opportunity. I was three weeks into my new job and was taking a day off to drive with my middle daughter to see my parents. On our drive south, I needed to stop by my office to pick up my first paycheck. After cajoling her into joining me, Aly, seventeen, followed me through the shiny glass doors of my office building. I took her to the cafeteria, as my dad had done, and offered her breakfast that was turned down with a wave of her hand.

Once upstairs, we walked down the narrow aisle between cubicles and stopped at the desk of one of my employees. I paused and said, "Aly, I would like you to meet Craig." Aly shook his hand with confidence as I continued. "Craig has been so helpful getting me up to speed here. I could never have ramped up this fast without him." We couldn't help but notice his eyes light up as we turned to walk away. When we got to my office, Aly turned to me and smiled.

"I know why you did that."

"Did what?" I said.

"You complimented him in front of me to make him feel good, didn't you? Just like Papa did when you were little," she said teasingly.

"I guess you are right. It never hurts to tell people how much you appreciate them. I had one of the best role models."

I imagine one day Aly will do the same. Leading and parenting are much like fraternal twins. They come from the same place in your heart and soul, and are intimately connected. While their outer shells may appear slightly different, they are emotionally and genetically tied. In both leading and parenting, it is our job to be role models of human kindness, authenticity, and gratitude. In fact, this intersection strikes me all the time. Here is a short blog I wrote a few months ago that brings this to life.

Cultivating Future Leaders

As a parent and as a leader, both for over twenty years, I have found myself looking for teaching moments in the home and in the office. I believe that we can nurture our children not only to be "good" people but also to be strong, thoughtful leaders. If we slow down enough in our hectic lives, we will find these seeds being planted all around us.

This weekend was a flurry of birthday activities for my ten-year-old daughter, the youngest of three girls with her sisters already off to college. With that history, I feel like I have seen it all—wizards, princesses, magicians, pottery, and picnics. The anxiety of planning the perfect birthday party far exceeds that of preparing for everyday business meetings. After countless suggestions were turned down with a rolling of the eyes, my daughter finally settled on bowling. Phew! By the time the invitations were out, we had just over a week to spare before the party date.

Fast forward to the party, where the girls gathered with electric energy on a blustery and rainy day. Even at the age of ten, these girls already show signs of leadership, collaboration, negotiation, and inspiration. To my surprise, tears were not shed following defeat—rather the girls cheered each other on to personal victories. If you stop long enough to notice the behavior, you see that this is what we should be modeling at work. Rather than judging each other and encouraging corporate politics, we should be inspiring others to thrive.

Finally, when my daughter opened her gifts, the card that accompanied the first one stunned me. "Thank you so much for inviting me to your b-day. You are a great friend and I want to encourage our friendship. You are always kind and inclusive. You share so much of your stuff with me and I'm very thankful for that!" Ten years old! Fast-forward twenty years to the workplace and imagine how that might play out. The seeds of leadership are planted at an early age. Slow down a little bit each day, and you will see our future leaders at play.

No matter where I turn, these magic moments are teaching me lessons. I am constantly reminded that I am one person—not a mom and a friend and a boss and a daughter and a "fill in the blank"—I am *me*. Living authentically means that you don't have to create artificial barriers in order to appear this way or that way depending on your audience. You are free to be whoever you are without worrying who others want you to be. One of the greatest gifts I have received in the last few years is the understanding that authenticity is freedom.

"Often misconstrued, authenticity is not about being an open book, revealing every detail of yourself without rhyme or reason. It is simply the act of openly and coura- geously seeing what needs to be seen, saying what needs to be said, doing what needs to be done, and becoming that which you are intent on being."

– SCOTT EDMUND MILLER, *The User's Guide to Being Human: The Art* and *Science of Self*

CHAPTER FIVE

Decide, Declare,
and Do What it Takes

*"'Are you sure, Gray?' He lifted his eyes. 'No... I'm not.
I'm not sure of a damn thing.' He slipped his hands
free of the monsignor's and peeled the battery off
the phone, cutting the last ring in half.
'But that doesn't mean I won't act.'"*

– JAMES ROLLINS, *The Judas Strain*

Deciding. Should I or shouldn't I, do I or don't I? While facing an infinite array of daily choices is a fact of life, wrestling with delaying decision making until being certain of a positive outcome has plagued me for as long as I can remember. I realize many others experience this as well, and the irony is, being obsessed with making the "correct" decision often means becoming paralyzed by an inability to be at peace with our choice. So, we make no decisions at all. Zippo. Nada.

After finally *deciding* to get divorced, I gradually came to learn that it is "the deciding" that sets us free. When we make a decision, we are no longer stuck. Only then can we begin to move *toward* something. Most of the time we have no idea what awaits us at the other end of the decision, but after years of reading and learning and thinking and pausing (yes, I am tired), I finally realized that it doesn't matter *what* is on the other side. The other side holds as many infinite possibilities as the decision itself, and in waiting to make a choice, we are only delaying realization of the joy that will ultimately result. I run the risk of losing you here with this heady discussion, so I will illustrate my point with a story.

I had been working at the same job for nearly three years when I decided it was time to make a change. Just deciding it was time for a change was not enough because it is not only important to decide what we are going to do, but also to declare it. While I couldn't let my colleagues know that I was looking for a new job, I did hint to those outside of my company that I was seeking a change. It wasn't simply that I *wanted* a change, I decided I *needed* a change. Making that decision and declaration meant that I had to do whatever was necessary. I wasn't going to get a new job just by thinking about it and keeping it to myself. It was up to me to make it happen. I had learned that this is part of mental toughness, so I was not backing down.

In deciding to find a new job, it was uncanny how the job ended up finding me. Before I knew it, executive search firms were making inquiries. Had they been making inquiries all along and I just hadn't noticed? Did making the decision somehow open my eyes to things I had not seen that were right in front of me? It's like thinking about a car you want to buy, and then seeing it *everywhere*. You think your idea is so unique, yet, once thought, it so often becomes obvious that this is not the case.

This is the power of *thinkronicity*. Think it and it will be. While synchronicity, according to Merriam Webster's dictionary, is "the coincidental occurrence of events and especially psychic events (as similar thoughts in widely separated persons or a mental image of an unexpected event before it happens) that seem related but are not explained by conventional mechanisms of causality," thinkronicity is the thinking of a person, place, or event that causes the coincidental occurrence itself.

The decision to get a new job made possible the actualization of finding one.

"*If you obsess over whether you are making the right decision, you are basically assuming that the universe will reward you for one thing and punish you for another.*

The universe has no fixed agenda. Once you make any decision, it works around that decision. There is no right or wrong, only a series of possibilities that shift with each thought, feeling, and action that you experience.

If this sounds too mystical, refer again to the body. Every significant vital sign—body temperature, heart rate, oxygen consumption, hormone level, brain activity, and so on—alters the moment you decide to do anything ... decisions are signals telling your body, mind, and environment to move in a certain direction."

– DEEPAK CHOPRA, *The Book of Secrets:*
Unlocking the Hidden Dimensions of Your Life

CHAPTER SIX

Be the Change

*"Everyone thinks of changing the world, but
no one thinks of changing himself."*

– LEO TOLSTOY

In times of change and uncertainty, it is often easiest to just sit and do nothing while we wait for the tide to turn, or for someone else to make decisions for us. The thought of making a choice, or doing anything for that matter, is daunting and overwhelming beyond description. Why can't everyone and everything around me change so that I don't have to?

It is human nature to want to change others to fit our needs, or our image of what is valuable, but this desire so often leads to broken relationships, shame, and feelings of unworthiness. What I have discovered is that in being the change ourselves, the relationships we have can magically morph into something amazing and new.

I am reminded here of Father's Day weekend with my mom in 2015, which in the days before, I was anticipating with cautious optimism. I stress the word cautious, as I wasn't sure of how I would handle my mother's feelings and uncertainty around Dad's health. How would I be able to relate to her loneliness? After all, she and my father had been married for fifty-five years—after beginning to date when she was only thirteen! My relationship, which didn't hold a candle to theirs, had ended in divorce.

On this particular weekend, Mom and I would be spending time alone together in her home for the first time ever. And I do mean ever. There had never been one without the other … my mother without my father, or my father without my mother. While Dad was still living, he was no longer residing in the house they had shared, and I wasn't sure how I would handle being the only person standing between my mother and her grief.

Months prior to my father's move into a nursing home, when I had visited for just twenty-four hours, I hadn't known how to handle my mother's sadness. I had done my best to stay above her pain, believing if I didn't talk about it maybe it would just go away. What resulted was far worse than if I had faced it head on, and my efforts to remain on the surface prevented me from being there for her. I unconsciously put pressure on Mom to be grateful that Dad was still alive, grateful for having had so many happy years together. I was asking her to do all of the hard work, asking her to change. She even called me on it, requesting that I just listen.

Returning to Father's Day weekend 2015—and my concern about falling into the same trap—what transpired was something short of a miracle. When I stepped through the big, weathered-pine front door, my petite, blue-eyed mother greeted me with a huge smile. We hugged tightly and each let out a sigh of relief. From that moment on, we shared, we laughed, we loved. We told countless stories about my childhood, about her childhood, about everything. Most of all, we celebrated my father's life, and Mom spoke in detail of her love for him. Her eyes welled up with tears as she recounted romantic stories of their courtship. I listened. I held her hand as we sat on the soft leather couch that had been my dad's post for the last five years, where they used to sit and hold hands just as my mom and I were doing in that moment. Upon reflection, I realized that this was what I should have done months ago, allowing my mom the space to sit with her feelings. By changing my approach to her instead of trying to change her, we set the stage for a magical weekend. As we stood up from the couch, she held my hands in hers, looked directly into my eyes and said, "I didn't know that I could ever feel this happy again. I guess I was wrong."

CHAPTER SEVEN

Let it Go

The wind is howling like this swirling storm inside
Couldn't keep it in;
Heaven knows I've tried

Don't let them in,
don't let them see
Be the good girl you always have to be

Conceal, don't feel,
don't let them know
Well now they know

Let it go, let it go

– Frozen, **Disney** Films

Many of us have an idealized image of how we think we should be, which is why I spent much of my life hiding behind a brick wall hoping to prevent the world from seeing what I perceived to be weaknesses. During our formative years, many of us learn that vulnerability is weakness, and that weakness is unattractive. These impressions and misperceptions, hardwired into our brains, are often responsible for pesrsistent feelings of unworthiness. We strive to be good enough, smart enough, thin enough, rich enough, this enough and that enough. I always believed that if I could achieve perfection, I would be "happy." The reality, thanks to what I now know, is far different. As Brené Brown wrote in *Daring Greatly*, "Perfectionism is a self-destructive and addictive belief system that fuels this primary thought: If I look perfect and do everything perfectly, I can avoid or minimize the painful feelings of shame, judgment, and blame."

When we come face to face with uncertainty, we are forced to question our belief system, and it may become a struggle to move forward. By hiding behind a shield of perfectionism, we think no one will see our shortcomings, but I am here to tell you that it is in letting go that we will experience miracles and magic. When we shine a light on the shadow, it disappears. We create light where new life can grow. Shame and pain seem to grow in the darkness, yet when light is shone on that same darkness, feelings of worthiness and joy flourish.

One of the hardest things I have ever done was shine the light on my personal struggle with irritable bowel syndrome (IBS). Who wants to talk about their bowels? It is not great table conversation, yet when you live with it day in and day out, it is hard to avoid. Plagued with this condition for over thirty years, I carried an unbearable weight of shame and embarrassment. I had been repeatedly told IBS was caused by emotional stress, but was I really so stressed at age eleven? There had to be some other cause. It seemed the medical community was trying to explain the unexplainable when they told me I just had to live with it and manage my anxiety. For years I accepted this, until it was so bad that I could barely function.

Snapshots

"I'm afraid that your irritable bowel syndrome has progressed. You now have furious and vindictive bowel syndrome."

In 2010, when my symptoms became so extreme that getting to work was impossible without numerous stops at gas stations along the way, I had lost so much weight my colleagues thought I was suffering from a life-threatening disease. At that time, my self-care consisted of a combination of starvation and medicating with over-the-counter drugs.

Thinking back on this difficult period, I realize it was by coming out from hiding that I was able to treat the disease that was ravaging my body. When I finally shared what was going on with a friend—who thankfully told me about a health care provider specializing in "leaky" gut—I was a shell of a woman shaking from malnourishment and stress.

As my first appointment with the nutritionist began, I broke down in tears, pleading for relief. She compassionately listened to my story, and then mapped out my journey to health. The next six months consisted of unraveling the mystery of my gut by identifying food intolerances and sensitivities. Every meal was an effort and fraught with fear, so I ate a strict gluten-free, dairy-free, sugar-free, and fun-free diet. There was no hiding my IBS. Imagine sitting at a professional dinner and explaining why you have ordered a "special meal." Talk about shining the light on the darkness! I had a huge spotlight that followed me wherever I went, but what I learned is I am not alone in my suffering (shockingly, one in seven people suffer from IBS). In sharing my experience, I have also been able to help others heal, which has allowed me to let go of a lifetime of embarrassment about having this condition. As I came out of the shadows by shining the light on IBS, an awakening helped me create new neurological pathways that have done away with shame and self-judgment.

Let it go. Yes, just let it go. When I made the decision to let go, I was blessed with magic around me making it easier. There was no going back.

She Let Go

She let go. Without a thought or a word, she let go.
She let go of the fear.
She let go of the judgments.
She let go of the confluence of opinions swarming
  around her head.
She let go of the committee of indecision within her.
She let go of all the "right" reasons.
Wholly and completely, without hesitation or worry,
  she just let go.
She didn't ask anyone for advice.
She didn't read a book on how to let go.
She didn't search the scriptures.
She just let go.
She let go of all of the memories that held her back.
She let go of all of the anxiety that kept her from moving
  forward.
She let go of the planning and all of the calculations
  about how to do it just right.
She didn't promise to let go.
She didn't journal about it.
She didn't write the projected date in her Day-Timer.
She made no public announcement and put no ad in the
  paper.
She didn't check the weather report or read her
  daily horoscope.
She just let go.

She didn't analyze whether she should let go.
She didn't call her friends to discuss the matter.
She didn't do a five-step Spiritual Mind Treatment.
She didn't call the prayer line.
She didn't utter one word.
She just let go.
No one was around when it happened.
There was no applause or congratulations.
No one thanked her or praised her.
No one noticed a thing.
Like a leaf falling from a tree, she just let go.
There was no effort.
There was no struggle.
It wasn't good and it wasn't bad.
It was what it was, and it is just that.
In the space of letting go, she let it all be.
A small smile came over her face.
A light breeze blew through her. And the sun
and the moon shone forevermore ...

– Rev. Safire Rose

CHAPTER EIGHT

Heal from the Inside Out

*"Everything you'll ever need to know is within you;
the secrets of the universe are imprinted on the cells
of your body. But you haven't learned how to read the
wisdom of the body. So you can only read books and
listen to experts and hope they are right."*

– DAN MILLMAN, *Way of the Peaceful Warrior*

Facing the realities of my physical gut forced me to examine my emotional gut as well. There was clearly a tie between my mind and my body that was impacting my health. It wasn't enough to just treat the symptoms of IBS, and I was convinced that my physical malady had its roots in something deeper.

My nutritionist referred me to a woman who ran a practice specializing in the Emotional Freedom Technique (EFT). With a name like that, how could I go wrong?

Dr. Joseph Mercola describes EFT as "... a form of psychological acupressure, based on the same energy meridians used in traditional acupuncture to treat physical and emotional ailments for over five thousand years, but without the invasiveness of needles. Instead, simple tapping with the fingertips is used to input kinetic energy onto specific meridians on the head and chest while you think about your specific problem—whether it is a traumatic event, an addiction, pain, etc.—and voice positive affirmations."

I had been in and out of traditional therapy since I was sixteen and decided to give this alternative a try. What I experienced was something just shy of a miracle. Admittedly, I was skeptical as I walked up the weathered wooden stairs to the office nestled alongside the San Francisco Bay. The sun was especially bright, and upon reflection, I realize now it must have been a sign.

When I entered the office, a tall, elegant woman greeted me with an extended hand that held mine with warmth and comfort. She began our session by confirming the reason for my visit, and I quickly settled into an aura of safety. Within a matter of minutes, the therapist asked me to consider the possibility of my having had a traumatic childhood event that might have triggered any feelings of anxiety. In almost no time it hit me, and tears started pouring from my tired eyes.

The scent of the black leather interior of the old green Mercedes filled the air as if I was back in that car in 1978, a pre-teen sitting in the backseat wedged between the passenger door and my paternal grandfather's shoulder. My heart raced as I remembered that trapped feeling of fight or flight. His strong arm was draped around my shoulder as he slid his hand down my cotton turtleneck and brushed against my budding breast. It was all I could do not to scream and alert my parents, who were in the front seat, about the wrong that was being committed. But my voice was silent. I squirmed away from him, and as soon as we arrived at our destination, I leaped out of the car.

The calm in the EFT room brought me back to reality, and we sat in the silence of my discovery. Is that the trauma that triggered my IBS? I had not thought of this moment in over twenty years and yet, in this instant, it came to me like a bolt of lightening.

After six months of working with the EFT therapist, while also making important dietary modifications, I succeeded in healing my gut. The protective barrier I kept around me for all of those years had prevented me from confronting the pain of that violation. I had thought the only way to survive was to hide behind a wall of perfection and strength, but in allowing myself to be vulnerable, I was able to attack the demon that was literally eating away at my insides.

When faced with adversity, dig deep and shine the light on the darkness. In *Carry on Warrior, Thoughts on Life Unarmed*, Glennon Doyle Melton writes, "We're not often permitted to tell the truth in everyday life …we find out early that telling the whole truth makes people uncomfortable and is certainly not ladylike or likely to make us popular, so we learn to lie sweetly so that we can be loved."

In other words, we shield the world and ourselves from our own truth. In my case, I chose the shield of perfection to show the world that I was fine. Decades later, healing from the inside out gave me the strength I needed to drop the shield.

CHAPTER NINE

Find Magic

*"The middle is messy, but it's also
where the magic happens."*

– BRENÉ BROWN, *Rising Strong*

Indeed, the middle *is* messy when winding our way through the maze of uncertainty, but I discovered that digging through the wreckage provides space for magic to occur. Facing an uncertain future head-on provides us with the ability to see that a positive outcome is possible, and it becomes a more "reliable" unknown.

I have spent most of my life hiding behind an armor of doing and over-functioning rather than just being, and now realize my mom was more spiritually enlightened than I gave her credit. When I was young, keeping my room impeccably tidy with nothing (and I mean nothing!) out of order was the norm. Years later my mom told me that she sighed in relief when my always-clean room was messy because she took this as a sign that I was happy. When it was too clean, she worried that I was imposing order on my life and hiding behind the image of perfection. As I reflect back on those times, I truly believe that she was right.

A therapist I was seeing years ago used to suggest taking the time to stop doing and just roll around in the grass with my daughter. "What, are you kidding?" I thought to myself. If I stop and just be, I might feel something I don't want to feel. It might get messy, and no longer be as neat and tidy as I have always preferred.

I recently realized that I had passed this legacy on to my oldest daughter. But knowing what I do now, I am hoping to help her find the magic buried in the messy.

On this particular weekend, my plans had been turned upside down with the cancellation of an international work trip. Hearing news of budget cuts, and that I would be pulled from the trip, was devastating. I had planned to see my middle daughter at college on the way home, and to see my boyfriend as well. How could this be? My whole world felt shattered, and I sobbed like a baby in my chair. What do I do now?

My oldest daughter, Megan, happened to call in the midst of my emotional meltdown, and by the sound of her voice on the other end of the phone I could tell she was concerned. "Mom, what's wrong? Did something happen to Papa?" My tears had sent warning signals to her that something really bad must have happened to set off such a response, and in that moment, she put it all into perspective for me: A trip was cancelled. It was as simple as that. And no, my father hadn't died. Within minutes, she and I made plans to actually go and visit my dad, whom she had not seen in eighteen months. Pure magic! In the midst of the rubble of my cancelled trip, we were able to create an opportunity to spend time with my parents.

As soon as we hung up the phone, I wiped away the tears and called my mom. I told her of our desire to come and visit, and after convincing her that "no Mom, Megan won't think you have aged twenty years," and "no Mom, your house is not a mess," she let her excitement take over.

I knew that this would be a difficult trip for Megan as the last time she had seen my dad he was walking, living at home, feeding himself, laughing, talking, and still somewhat present. Megan's uncertainty as to what she would see once we got there was obvious in spite of her introspective demeanor. She had been having nightmares about Papa dying without her being able to say goodbye, so I knew the guilt was weighing heavily on her. Given the uncertainty of the lifespan for those with Lewy Body Dementia, you never know which visit will be your last. I knew that these thoughts had taken hold in Megan's twenty-year-old heart and mind.

It was an unseasonably sweltering hot day in California when we pulled into the long driveway of my mom's Tudor home. We entered the expansive foyer to find my tiny little mother standing with open arms to take in the warmth of her first-born granddaughter. Tears welled up in my eyes as I watched these 5'2" women hug tightly. It was hard to believe that I was watching my daughter and my mother, together, after nearly two years apart. Magic!

I can only imagine what must have been going on in Megan's head as she walked around the big house that was no longer filled with my larger than life father's energy. Instead, the neat and tidy house was quiet in a calm yet eerie way. What Megan likely didn't understand was how much her presence meant to my mom, and how her spirit filled that empty house with joy and love. There we stood, three generations of women, each experiencing the same moment in our own way.

After waking from a night of restless sleep due to the suffocating summer heat, I mentally prepared for the morning ahead at the nursing home where my father lives, reminding myself that Megan had not seen him for a year and half. The three of us drove in my father's car, the scent of his cologne ever so faint in the saddle brown leather seats, our conversation hovering on superficial topics like the weather and plans for the afternoon following our visit.

Upon entering the nursing facility, I took a deep breath and draped my arm around my mom's shoulder while holding onto my daughter's gentle hand. As we rounded the corner, the staff greeted us with warm smiles and waves. The double doors swung open and there was my dad, seated in his wheelchair in front of the communal television in the lounge area. They had dressed him in his Boston Red Sox sweatshirt in honor of our visit. His eyes lit up when he saw us, and I gave him a big hug. "Hi Dad. Don't you look handsome in your Red Sox sweatshirt? This is your eldest granddaughter, Megan. She came for a visit just to see you!"

Megan gave him a cautious yet sincere smile as she made limited eye contact. Lewy Body Dementia had mentally and physically crippled her once strong and invincible Papa. How does a young girl reconcile her own emotions with such an unfamiliar situation?

Thankfully, the awkward silence was broken when one of the aides invited us to another location for music and singing, but as soon as we parked my dad's wheelchair in the back of the room, Megan unexpectedly excused herself. My instinct told me that she was overwhelmed as she has never been one to share uncomfortable emotions with others, and certainly not in a public setting. When she returned, eyes red from crying, her emotional response was a welcome one to me as it meant that she was allowing herself to feel and to grieve. This is where I found the magic. From this moment on, Megan was present with my dad, having come to accept the new reality. She looked relieved now as she rubbed his shoulders and smiled and laughed with him.

Even in sadness, as we move forward in times of uncertainty, we can find magic just beneath the surface. By allowing ourselves to become vulnerable, in this case Megan succumbing to the pent up anxiety and fear about seeing my dad, we release a little bit of magic and get to experience deeper love, connection, and wholeheartedness. These are the moments I remember far more than major events in my life, as they are the ones that shape who we are and further validate what it means to be authentic and true to ourselves.

CHAPTER TEN

Choose Gratitude

*"The miracle of gratitude is that it shifts your
perception to such an extent that it
changes the world you see."*

– DR. ROBERT HOLDEN
Author of *Happiness NOW!*

When faced with uncertainty and fear, the easy fallback is to feel like a victim. "Why did this happen to me? What did I do to deserve this? Nothing ever goes my way." I fell into this vicious cycle of self-destruction in the early stages of my separation, but over time, I was able to rewrite my story and let go of shame and the victim mentality. The infusion of positive energy from healers, family, and friends transformed my lens, and I began to look for the silver lining rather than at the cloud itself. Like many other moments in the last four years, I found magic tucked beneath the darkness.

It was January 2015, and I had the luxury of a work from home day that allowed me to pick up my ten-year-old daughter from school. Even after child number three, I still enjoy the rush of seeing that precious, smiling after school face. Once Jordan got into the car, she opened the sunroof of our Toyota Highlander and then stood on the console to wave goodbye to her friends. As she did this, she leaned on the edge of the roof as I tugged at her leg to request that she get in and buckle up.

When she returned to her seat, and tried to close the sunroof, all we heard was a whirring sound. We moved the lever back and forth to no avail—it wouldn't budge. Needless to say, I was worried that we couldn't close it given that the weather report called for rain, but after giving Jordan my motherly lecture on being careful, I took a deep breath and pulled into the garage. I figured I would buy myself some time before pursuing a repair, and left the car there until the following week.

Eventually, I conjured up the nerve to call the dealership to get an estimate. The friendly service manager on the other end of the line said, "I'm sure it is just a cable that should cost no more than $150." Phew, disaster averted! I took the car to my trusted service center and awaited a call with the final estimate. I was leaving town the next morning and was eager to get this off my plate.

The entire Saturday had flown by until just before six, when I missed the call and received a voicemail instead: "Hello, Ms. Slater. This is Dave from Toyota. I wanted to let you know that your car repair will be $1800. It appears that the motor mechanism needs to be replaced, and we can have it done next week with your authorization."

After listening to the message, I stood in shock for a few

minutes. Are you kidding me? I had just invested $1000 in the engine, the last thing I needed was to spend another $1800!!! I snapped out of it, immediately called the dealership, but could not reach the service manager. After several tries, I finally left a message stating that I would NOT authorize service, and they would have to keep my car for the week as I was heading out of town.

How could my little ten-year-old wreak this kind of havoc? But then again, what was I to do? Blaming her was certainly not going to pay the bill.

Fast forward five days, and I was packing to come home from a hectic week at a conference in Las Vegas (I know, a hectic week there conjures up all sorts of imagery), but nonetheless, I was heading home when I received a call from an oddly familiar, unidentified number on my cell phone. With hesitation, I answered the call in my usual tone.

"Hello, this is Amy."

"Hi, Amy. This is Jane from the Toyota dealership in Marin."

Immediately, I went on the defensive. "Oh, hi Jane. I am so sorry that I have not been in to pick up my car. I have been out of town and can come in tomorrow morning to retrieve it."

"Well, you can certainly come to pick it up tomorrow, as it has been repaired."

A long pause was made even longer due to my shock over the fact that they had repaired the car without my approval. I was ready to launch into a complaint when she broke the silence.

"You see, there was a little miscommunication this week and your car was mistakenly repaired. Another car was in for a similar service and the technician repaired yours by accident. Since you did not authorize the work, we cannot charge you for it."

I tried to tame my enthusiasm over this miraculous news. I had no idea how I was going to have the car fixed, as I did not want to invest $1800 in a second family vehicle with over 150,000 commute miles. My response was one of sheer gratitude for their integrity and superior service. Jane did not even suggest that I pay a dime for the work; rather she thanked me for being such a loyal customer and asked for nothing in return.

The next day when I went to pick up the car, my effusiveness filled the dealership. Gestures like this remind me that human decency and fairness do exist; that I should not play the victim when I think life is unfair; that nice people don't always finish last; and, finally, it reminds me to slow down enough to let the Universe decide how best to take care of me.

In the early pages of this book I stated "It seemed that 'someone' (I will tell you who later) was pointing me in a new direction." That someone is the Universe, and I have found faith in things larger than life as I know it. This is not to discount anyone else's belief in religion, Gods and Goddesses, spiritual leaders and teachers, or any other source. I have learned to trust the unwritten plan for my life, and to choose gratitude as my companion.

CHAPTER ELEVEN

Love Unconditionally

*"Love—not dim and blind but so far-seeing that
it can glimpse around corners, around bends and
twists and illusion; instead of overlooking faults love
sees through them to the secret inside."*

– VERA NAZARIAN, *Salt of the Air*

During times of uncertainty it is common to turn inward and become paralyzed by our fear of the unknown. We protect ourselves from further disappointment by retreating, and our insecurity thus perpetuates itself.

Instead of turning inside with judgment and self-doubt, we need to love ourselves without condition. How often do you look inside and think you are not good enough, or smart enough, or rich enough? I know I was paralyzed by the belief that I was unlovable. How could anyone love me? I failed my marriage and ruined my daughters' lives (or so I thought). This self-blame common in so many of us only fuels uncertainty, making it all the more difficult to move forward.

While on the phone with my mom recently, I was reminded of special moments in my life when I felt true, unconditional love. We were discussing my blessed maternal grandmother, Mildred Monson, who was born in 1912 in a small Kansas town. Her radiant smile lit up the room like sunlight on a clear day, which I noticed even as young as age six. Dooey, as we called her, was loved by everyone, but heart disease took her from this earth when she was only sixty-two.

As a young girl, the highlight of my weekend was sleeping over at Dooey's West Los Angeles high-rise apartment. She would drive my sister and I to Nibblers, a local diner, in her sporty white Thunderbird with bright red leather interior. Spending time with her was magical. I can still remember her soft, fair hands as she reached out to hold mine while crossing the street. She always introduced me with such warmth and pride, and let me order Coke in the old-fashioned glass bottles and take a handful of Ande's mint candies on my way out. Moments like these are engraved in my heart. I never doubted her feelings for me as she was always present, always kind, and loved me tenderly, without condition.

If she could love me unconditionally, why couldn't I love myself that way? Unconditional love provides the connections that we all need to feel valued and safe. As a parent, I worry that my daughters will have their own self-doubts. How will it be possible to teach them self-love if I struggle with it myself?

I have one daughter left at home and feel as if every day is another lesson, although I sometimes fantasize about turning down the volume of my awakening and floating above the fray for just a short while. However, as I have said before, once you see you can no longer "un-see," and at times it feels like an out of body experience to parent my youngest child.

At ten years old, Jordan is struggling with the concept of mortality. Not only that, but she is faced with comings and goings each week as she transitions between my house and her father's, just three miles away. Recently, she started saying "I love you" every fifteen minutes or so. If I don't respond within twenty seconds, she repeats herself, but with a question in her voice, so I quickly say I love you back. If I ever have a blank look on my face or am not smiling, she'll say, "I love you," and if I act disappointed in her she'll quickly say it as well.

After weeks of this, I started to change my response. Instead of saying "I love you" back, I said, "Jordan, are you worried that my love is conditional? Just because I say I am disappointed in your behavior doesn't mean that I don't love you. My love is unconditional. I love you no matter what." This seemed to make sense to her, yet she continued to check in regularly to make sure that I do indeed love her.

Finally, I asked her again if she was feeling okay, and she began to cry, explaining that she was worried about something happening to me. Saying "I love you" is her way of staying connected to me, and if for any reason I don't come back from a business trip or from work one day, she will know that those were our last words.

How can I argue with that? How can I refute her desire to remain connected with three simple words? She addresses her uncertainty through establishing a connection, while most adults address uncertainty by running away or hiding. It takes courage to tackle uncertainty; it takes courage to come out of hiding. As kids we used to say Ollie ollie oxen free during games like hide and seek or capture the flag to indicate all who are "out" may come in without penalty. Little did I know what a valuable phrase it would become for me as an adult, and I've now learned it's okay to come out and face uncertainty—we won't be penalized.

CHAPTER TWELVE

Stand for Something

"If you stand for something you will have people for you and people against you. But if you stand for nothing you will have nobody for you and nobody against you."

– MAURICE SAATCHI

Midway through my career I learned the importance of developing a personal and professional brand thanks to the encouragement of a mentor. I am grateful for this advice as, up until then, I assumed promotions and recognition would be based upon my hard work and sales performance. Little did I realize that performance alone would not pave the road to my success; I was naïve to think that others felt as strongly about me as I did. Thankfully, my mentor set me straight and advised me to lobby for myself. In order to do that, I needed to establish a brand and stand for something.

It was a struggle to figure out what I stood for, but after brainstorming for a while I came up with a list of characteristics that I thought made me a viable candidate for promotion.

As a result of this effort, I created a one-page document that was much more than a resume, which I proceeded to share with other mentors who could help promote me to leaders outside of my own organization. When forced to define what I stood for, I was able to stare my career uncertainty right in the face. Prior to that, I had blamed the system for my having been overlooked for new positions. I blamed, made excuses, and then hid behind my protective wall.

As I moved on from Cisco, I became a huge advocate of building one's own brand. When you stand for something, you remove uncertainty. You build trust. What you see is what you get.

At this point you may be wondering about the word "martinis" in the title of this book. When I was struggling with the lowest point of my IBS, I had to remove alcohol from my diet completely. After a year without drinking, I decided to bring a little liquid refreshment back into my repertoire, and having been introduced to potato vodka, I opted to pair that with olive juice—lots of olive juice. Of course, one cannot order a vodka martini with lots of olive juice without asking for an "extra dirty vodka martini," so, when at a business dinner and the waiter asked, "Ma'am, what can I get you to drink?" I replied in a whisper, "I'd like an extra dirty, vodka martini."

Leaning in closer, the waiter said, "I'm sorry. Can you repeat that?"

Taking a deep breath, I was forced to state with confidence, "I would like an EXTRA DIRTY vodka martini." Heads turned at the tables nearby, and I smiled and said, "I like them dirty. Extra dirty."

Now, when I meet friends for dinner or drinks, there is often an extra dirty potato vodka martini waiting there just for me.

This was one of the experiences that helped me learn not to be afraid to stand for something, even when it means a moment of embarrassment—it sure beats sitting behind the wall of shame trying to find the courage to stand up and face the uncertain road ahead.

CHAPTER THIRTEEN

Move Toward

"You have to take the view that there is nothing wrong with you; you are okay; you can allow this feeling to be there; you can 'lean in to the sharp points' ..."

– PEMA CHODRON, *Fail, Fail Again, Fail Better*

When preparing to write this final chapter, I noticed signs all around validating my improved approach to facing adversity and uncertainty, including when Pema Chodron's new book jumped off the shelf, and I had to stop what I was doing to read it—the irony here being that the subtitle of her book was simply another way of stating mine.

When Pema Chodron spoke at her daughter's college commencement ceremony, she shared her perspective on failure, describing how much value we derive from learning how to fail. Her recommendation to "lean into the unknown," to take steps to move toward what it is you want, is really that simple.

Human instinct tells us to run away when we are scared, so we retreat, hide, build walls—all to protect ourselves from the unknown. Over the past four years, the Universe has shown me something far different. After knocking down the protective barrier around my heart, I was able to see what I had never seen before. The wall had kept others from seeing me, but it had also kept me from seeing out. There were no windows in this wall. While I thought I was building a safe place to hide, I was doing quite the opposite. I had prevented myself from experiencing the growth that results from learning how to deal with the inevitable uncertainties that life brings.

Once that wall came down, it was as if someone had turned up the stereo to maximum volume, and I couldn't help but see the world through a different lens. The cloak of shame no longer had a place around my shoulders, having been replaced by wonder, curiosity, and self-reflection. I now understood that we have the power to tell our story as we want to; we have the power to choose our own future. We are what we create.

It is easy to dismiss the magic that I have shared as just "hocus-pocus," but I am living proof that this mysterious power is within reach—as long as we slow down long enough to capture it.

As a result, once we let go enough, we can see the magic in each moment and can never "un-see" it.

Moving toward what we want activates what is needed for fulfillment of that desire. The how's and the what's will not always be clear, and while the tendency may be to wait until you know exactly how you are going to get there, just take that first step. Don't wait. The rest will then have an opportunity to unfold with grace and ease.

Stop complaining. Slow down. Be authentic. Decide, declare, and do what it takes. Be the change. Let it go. Heal from the inside out. Find magic. Choose gratitude. Love unconditionally. Stand for something. Move toward.

The Beginning

Moments:
Journal Entries

Cinderella Fantasy (winter, 2011)

Hard to describe the loss I feel.
Must have been some Cinderella fantasy.
The clock struck 12 and my prince was gone.
Awakening from that dream, I don't know how to heal.

I look inside and am not sure what I see.
Pain takes over and happiness is a distant memory.
Struggling to find myself each day.
I only know how to do, not to be.

Must have been a Cinderella fantasy
Always longing for the fairytale dream.
Let me stop doing; let me be
Let me be, let me be, oh fairy Godmother, let me be.

Peeling away the layers of the past
Seeing my reflection in the present.
Where will my journey of discovery take me?
How many days will the suffering last?

My heart starts to open and my steps get lighter
Perhaps there is a way to move on
Surrounded by love and friendship
Indeed the future is becoming brighter.

Must have been a Cinderella fantasy.
Always longing for the fairytale dream.
Let me stop doing; let me be.
Let me be, let me be, oh fairy Godmother, let me be.

A fantasy, yes, a Cinderella Fantasy, a Cinderella Fantasy.
Oh fairy Godmother, let me be.

Two Worlds *(winter, 2011)*

I wake up in the morning and what do I see but two worlds
glaring up at me.
Two worlds that give me life; worlds that make me ME.
Treading ever so lightly to avoid the cracks in the ground
My head keeps spinning round and round.
Where will they take me, these worlds of mine and keep
me safe so that I am fine?

Two worlds keeping me together
Two worlds opening doors to another place
To a place where I can be free, truly free to let me, be me.

You told me it would be okay to let go and now you tell
me that isn't so.
Push me, pull me, which end is up?
I thought we agreed to never let go.
You let go and I hold tighter, and I let go and you become
a fighter.

Two worlds keeping me together
Two worlds opening doors to another place
To a place where I can be free, truly free to let me, be me.

*Finding a place where love can grow is becoming harder
than you know.
Letting go of the pain inside and the memories that I
wish I could hide.
How do I do it? How do I move on from this place inside?
The place with the scars; the impressions of you and me
together
When I thought it would be forever.*

*Two worlds keeping me together
Two worlds opening doors to another place
To a place where I can be free, truly free to let me be me.*

An Unnatural State *(winter, 2012)*

5:30 AM the alarm goes off. I don't really need an alarm since I awaken every morning at 3 AM. I toss and turn until 5:30 AM when I actually have to get up. I used to get up at 5:30 AM to work out, but now I get up early to get ready before I have to get the kids ready for school. I shower, make lunches, do laundry, empty the dishwasher and then at 6:30, I wake up the girls. Most people are still slumbering at this hour.

I turn over to see the stack of pillows next to me. These are the pillows that always came between us. He would often say, as many men do, "Why do we have so many**$%@& pillows on the bed? What purpose do they serve?" These pillows now remind me I am ALONE.

I walk in to the bathroom and look in the mirror. I am alone. I AM alone. I am ALONE. I am alone. Intellectually it feels good; emotionally it sucks. Things always come in pairs. We are not created to be alone. Adam and Eve. Peanut Butter and Jelly. Salt and Pepper. Bacon and Eggs. You and Me. Now, it is just me. I am not sure I remember who "me" is and how to be content with my singular self.

I play my music, turn on the light and sing as I get dressed. Dressing for work is like dressing for the stage. To the world, I have always led the "perfect" life. Who would think any differently when I hide behind the façade of confidence, strength and style? But, today, I cannot hide. I cannot hide the 15 pounds that I have lost during this transition. I cannot hide the dark circles and bags under my eyes. I cannot hide the lifeless stride as I walk down the hall.

I am alone. Moments of reflection as to what went wrong blindside me every day. I see a family walking together holding hands; or a man and a woman in an embrace. That is no longer me. I am in an Unnatural State.

Tomorrow —Ode to a Friend (summer, 2014)

Morning comes with a cape of fear
Heart races and dizziness sets in

How can you shake this feeling
A cloud of dread hangs above.

Through the crack in the door
Light sneaks in.

A slight breeze through the open window
A bird singing in the neighboring tree.

There is a new day
A better day
A happier day
Just ahead.

Lean in
Breathe
Breathe and
Breathe again.

Imagine arms holding you
It will be okay
You will be okay

The pain will subside
In time
I promise.
The pain will subside.

Tomorrow will bring peace
Tomorrow will be okay.
Tomorrow, you, will be okay.

Father's Day Tribute to John Reynolds Van Atta

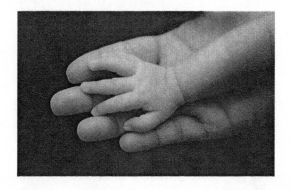

First memories of you...

Laughter, safety, gentle soul. I hold your leg in the grocery store; I look up and it is not you. Never want to lose you.

Holding hands everywhere we go. My small hand enveloped in your big, strong one. Little fingers wrapped around your hand so tight.

Picnics on the Lifeguard station; watching the planes come in while we eat our split pea soup and sandwiches. Where did the time go?

Halloween nights trick or treating around the Palisades. Homemade costumes. The best on the block.

Westlake Father Daughter dances. Practiced dancing on toes and now this was the real thing. Beaming with pride, with you, Dad, by my side.

Being dropped off at UC Berkeley for my college adventure. Tears, fears and soggy goodbyes.

You prepared me for this thing called Life. You gave me my emotional and intellectual arsenal to make it through.

Following in your management footsteps. You, my role model for success. The "One Minute Manager," confidante and friend.

I learned from you the foundation of relationships: trust, love and mutual respect. A lesson you taught me many times. I think I've got it now.

Children, parenting, love and understanding. Lead by example. Love by example.

You are the definition of hard work, passion, brilliance, love and selflessness.

You are MY DAD!!!

I love you and wish I could be there to celebrate you!
xoxo
Amy

RESOURCES

In Print

Paulo Coelho, *The Alchemist*

Glennon Doyle Melton, *Carry on, Warrior: Thoughts on Life Unarmed*

Don Miguel Ruiz, *The Four Agreements*

Brené Brown, *The Gifts of Imperfection*

Brené Brown, *Daring Greatly*

Katrina Mayer, *The Mustard Seed Way*

David R. Hawkins, *Power vs. Force*

"Discovering Your Authentic Leadership," Bill George, Peter Sims, Andrew N. McLean, and Diana Mayer. *Harvard Business Review* 85, no. 2 (February 2007)

Scott Edmund Miller, *The User's Guide to Being Human: The Art and Science of Self*

James Rollins, *The Judas Strain*

Deepak Chopra, *The Book of Secrets: Unlocking the Hidden Dimensions of Your Life*

Dr. Robert Holden, *Happiness NOW!, Shift Happens!, Authentic Success*, www.robertholden.org

Vera Nazarian, *Salt of the Air*

Pema Chodron, *Fail, Fail Again, Fail Better*

Online

Brené Brown: www.ted.com/talks brene_brown_on_vulnerability? language=en

Chris Dorris: www.christopherdorris.com

Essentials for Health (IBS): www.essentialsforhealth.info

Kinetic Waves (EFT): www.kineticwaves.com

ABOUT THE AUTHOR

As an SVP of a leading technology company, highly sought after leadership mentor, keynote speaker and parent, Amy Van Atta Slater, through her insights on life, business, personal development, parenting and mindfulness, has inspired thousands of business professionals and creative thinkers to adjust, rethink and refocus in every field and walk of life.

After graduating from the University of California at Berkeley, Amy soon became a noted leader in business, and 25 years later, she is consistently inspiring others towards greater levels of success. Motivating the masses with galvanizing speeches, Amy empowers others to build their brands and lead through the cultivation of culture. As a corporate strategy advisor and private executive mentor, Amy cultivates the development of core leadership skills combined with compassion, mindfulness and authenticity. Her unique approach to leadership development has garnered Amy coveted keynote speaking opportunities, such as the 2014 Forrester Research Convention, as a panelist at the Domo Women in Business Tour and as a featured speaker at the 2016 Apttus Accelerate conference in San Francisco.

Passionate about her responsibilities as a parent, Amy brings her message home modeling resilience, strength, authenticity, compassion and gratitude for her three daughters.

Contact Amy through her website
www.amyvslater.com

Read the first chapter of Amy's upcoming book:

Moments 2.0

Chauffeurs, Chivalry and Champagne
Are they Really Dead?

Amy Van Atta Slater

INTRODUCTION

In my first book, I shared my stories about the magic and miracles that I uncovered on my journey of awakening. Upon reflection, I don't want you thinking that it wasn't without trials and tribulations. What I intentionally did not write about was the topic of romantic love and connection. I also realized that I wanted to write a book to let all of you know YOU ARE NOT ALONE. While being single has its perks, it also has its pain. The pain, however, is where we learn and where we heal. We cry, like I have done many times, but we also must find time to laugh and laugh and laugh again. Thankfully, I have learned that I cannot take myself too seriously. After all, I only have one life to live in this mind and this body.

As I did in *Moments: Magic, Miracles, and Martinis*, I am going to take you on a journey, but this time, the journey will be through the windshield of a shiny town car carefully driven by my favorite driver and now friend, Kerry (known to others as a chauffeur). This journey will twist and turn through the fog to the San Francisco International Airport. Please secure your seatbelt by lifting up the metal buckle and inserting the belt. In case of emergency, feel free to use your carry on item as a floatation device, unless of course you paid for one during online check-in.

CHAPTER ONE

Through the Fog

It seemed like a matter of minutes when we began rolling in the foothills before Oakland and suddenly reached a height and saw stretched out of us the fabulous white city of San Francisco on her eleven mystic hills with the blue Pacific and its advancing wall of potato-patch fog beyond, and smoke and goldenness in the late afternoon of time."
– JACK KEROUAC

Rolling over to the sound of my iphone alarm, I rubbed my eyes, put on my reading glasses (yes, I now require reading glasses for EVERYTHING) and saw the tiny numbers flashing 5AM. I looked outside my bedroom window only to see the hill blanketed with fog. Worries of flight delays swam around in my head as I imagined the back up that occurs for flights departing San Francisco International Airport (SFO). I turned on Pandora to my favorite morning music channel and went through my very early morning rituals.

Listening to music while I prepare for my day helps me set the stage for whatever lies ahead. On this particular morning, I was headed to LA for a simple two-day business trip. My car service was picking me up at 8 AM so I had ample time to prepare for the days ahead. I wondered with curious anticipation if Kerry would be my driver today or another on the roster of well-meaning journeymen.

Riding with Kerry was like being with family. He is familiar and full of life. His energy makes these frequent trips somewhat of a fantasy rather than the mundane reality that they can be. A gentle tap on the front door meant that I would soon find out who was transporting me through the fog. To my sheer delight, Kerry greeted me with his warm smile and heart-warming accent.

As I shut the door behind me, I headed down the steep driveway with an extra kick in my step. From that point, I knew that I was in for a ride.

Moments 2.0 will be published in early 2017.

NOTES

NOTES

NOTES

NOTES

NOTES

CPSIA information can be obtained
at www.ICGtesting.com
Printed in the USA
FSOW01n0217231017
40090FS

9 780997 070019